S0-DGJ-625

War in the Gulf

SADDAM HUSSEIN

Written By: Paul J. Deegan

Published by Abdo & Daughters, 6535 Cecilia Circle, Edina, Minnesota
55439.

Library bound edition distributed by Rockbottom Books, Pentagon Tower,
P.O. Box 36036, Minneapolis, Minnesota 55435.

Copyright © 1991 by Abdo Consulting Group, Inc., Pentagon Tower, P.O.
Box 36036, Minneapolis, Minnesota 55435. International copyrights
reserved in all countries. No part of this book may be reproduced in any
form without written permission from the publisher. Printed in the United
States.

Library of Congress Number: 91-073076   ISBN: 1-56239-025-2

Cover Photo by: UPI Bettmann
Inside Photos by: UPI Bettmann
                   Dept. of Defense: 25
                   Pictorial Parade: 4
                   Star Tribune: 19

Edited by: Rosemary Wallner

TABLE OF CONTENTS

Saddam Hussein, President of Iraq.

IRAQ'S LEADER

Saddam Hussein has been described in Western nations as a ruthless, cunning thug. In the early 1990s, Iraq's leader, it was said, wanted to dominate the Middle East and control the majority of the world's oil production.

After United States President George Bush began Operation Desert Shield in August 1990, he compared Saddam to Germany's Adolf Hitler. Hitler had wanted to take over much of Europe during World War II.

British Prime Minister John Major said Saddam was "amoral . . . a man without pity." "Whatever his fate may be," Major said, "I for one will not weep for him."

A Saudi prince said during Operation Desert Storm, launched in January 1991, that Saddam had "a pure criminal mentality, but now he is going crazy."

Who is this man who inspires such hostility?

Saddam Hussein was born April 28, 1937, in the Iraqi village of al Auja. The village is about 100 miles north of Baghdad, Iraq's capital. Saddam's father was a poor peasant. Saddam's home was a simple hut made of mud and reeds. There was no running water or electricity in his village. People burned cow dung for fuel.

Little is known of Saddam's early years. When he was young, his father apparently abandoned his family. Later his mother remarried. Saddam's stepfather was also an uneducated peasant. He did not like Saddam and treated him cruelly. He sent the boy to steal chickens and sheep which the stepfather then sold.

Because his stepfather opposed it, Saddam did not start school until 1947 when he was 10 years old. That year Saddam went to Baghdad to live with an uncle. The uncle, Khayrallah Tulfah, was a teacher who had been an army officer and later became mayor of Baghdad. Khayrallah hated the British and the influence of Western nations on Middle Eastern countries. Saddam listened to his uncle and soon adopted Tulfah's beliefs.

When he was 16 years old, Saddam finished junior high school. He wanted to become an army officer, but poor grades prevented him from entering the Baghdad Military Academy.

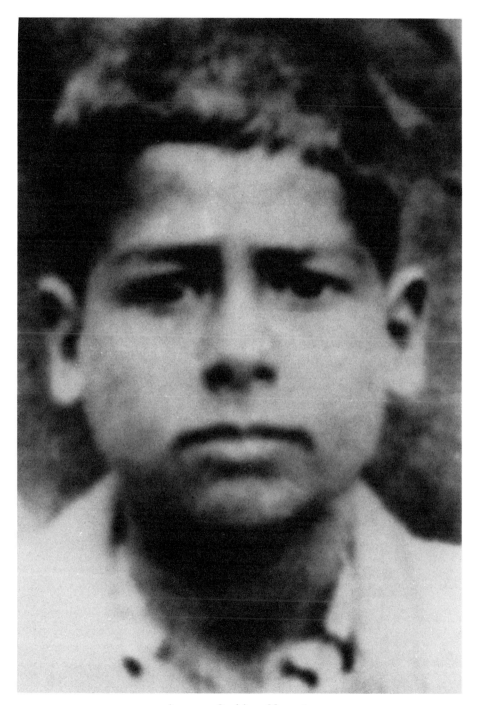

A young Saddam Hussein.

A TURBULENT IRAQ

The Iraq in which Saddam was born and grew up was very unstable politically. Conspiracy was the norm. The loyalties that most mattered in the Arab world were to family, tribe, and religion.

Iraq's history is filled with conflict between various ethnic, religious, and tribal groups. When Iraq gained its independence from Britain in 1932, the Iraq army emerged as the most powerful group in the country. In 1936, the army gained control of the government. The military's hold on the government remained a constant in 20th-century Iraq.

Iraq also was to be influenced by growing Arab nationalism. This movement got a large boost in the 1950s when Abdel Nasser led a revolt in Egypt. The revolt ousted Egypt's king. In 1956 Nasser stood off Britain, France, and Israel in a successful fight over control of the Suez Canal.

Five centuries of rule over Iraq by the Ottoman Turks had ended in 1917 when the British captured Iraq during World War I. The British controlled the country until 1920. Then the country was placed under a League of Nations mandate administered by the British. A year later

Iraq became a Hashemite kingdom. Iraq gained its independence in 1932.

In 1957, Saddam joined the Baath Party. He was 20 years old. The Baath Party was one of several radical nationalist parties appearing throughout the Arab world. The party favored an Arab brand of socialism. It wanted the government to control industries and ownership of land. The party was very anti-Western and anti-Israel. When Saddam became a member, the Baath in Iraq had few members and little influence.

The following year Iraq's King Faisal II was overthrown and assassinated. The government led by General Abdul Karim Qassim established a republic. A year later, the Baath tried to assassinate General Qassim. Saddam Hussein was part of the team sent to kill the general.

When the attempt to kill Qassim failed, Saddam fled to Syria. From there he went to Egypt and finished his high school education in Cairo at age 24. He remained active in Baathist politics and began law school in Cairo. He married his cousin, Sajida, in 1963 in Cairo. She was Khayrallah's daughter.

Saddam's student days ended in 1963 when Baathist army officers overthrew Iraq and killed

General Qassim. Saddam returned to Baghdad where he became an interrogator and torturer for the new regime.

The Baathists held power for only nine months. The party was still small and its members were divided. The Iraqi army drove the Baath from power. The army remained in control for the next five years.

SADDAM MOVES UP

Meanwhile Saddam had backed a leading Baathist. For his support, he was given a position in the party's ruling group. The once poverty-stricken peasant boy was on his way to wielding enormous power. The path to power, however, included over a year in prison. While imprisoned, Saddam decided he wanted to control the divided Baath party. He planned to create small groups loyal only to him.

He carried out his plan when he escaped from prison. He formed an internal security organization — the secret police. Among their tasks was executing the party's enemies. Saddam's rule by terror was underway.

In 1968, two years after his stay in jail, Saddam was involved in another Baathist takeover of the government. The Baath still had only about 5,000 members. But the party and officers of the army's Republican guards staged a successful coup on July 17.

The leading Baath military figure, General Ahmad Hassan al Bakr, became president of Iraq. The general was Saddam's cousin. Bakr also became commander in chief of the armed forces.

Bakr made Saddam, now 31, deputy chairman of the Baath Party's ruling Revolutionary Command Council. Saddam was placed in charge of internal security. He sent hundreds of men, including many of his relatives, to secret training schools. Saddam became, in effect, the number two man in Iraq. He was also using his position to gain control of the Baath Party so he could become number one.

He achieved this goal on July 16, 1979. On that date he declared himself president of Iraq, pushing aside the 64-year-old Bakr.

CONTROL BY TERROR

Saddam suspected that some of his friends and associates were not sympathetic to his takeover. He had five of them, including a close friend, arrested. The five soon confessed to plotting against Saddam. All of them, plus 17 others, were eventually executed.

After this, no one questioned whether or not Saddam should be the nation's ruler. His regime had shown it could suppress all opposition. Saddam was on his way to extending his government's grip far and wide.

"Saddam runs a ruthlessly efficient police state and an effective propaganda system," an American magazine reported during the Gulf crisis. His "personal control of the levers of power in his country is rivaled by only a few autocratic world leaders," wrote a newspaper reporter in 1991.

Since 1979 Saddam's rule by fear has extended into people's homes. His photo is displayed in many Iraqi living rooms. People do this because they don't want to be suspected of being disloyal to Saddam.

Like fellow-Baathist leader Hafez Assad in Syria, Saddam's rule is total. It relies on violent control of opponents. An expert on the Middle East said Saddam and Assad are not only "brutal," they are "smart." They have "no friends, only agents and enemies." The two men have created multiple security agencies. These agencies spy on the people, the army, and on each other. The vast internal security networks discourage any opposition.

Despite the many similarities between Saddam and Assad, the two dictators are bitter enemies.

ENEMIES ABOUND

Dictators are not without problems. One writer reported that Saddam thinks "the people all around him are trying to kill him." And there is good reason for that, the writer added, ". . . because, for much of his adult life, people all around him have been trying to kill him."

Saddam "did not finally get to be president of Iraq by being a nice guy," the writer noted. He survived in "a system that . . . punished the mild." While Saddam was murdering friends and enemies, he "made enough (enemies) to last several lifetimes."

Whenever Saddam leaves Iraq, he takes along his own food and food taster. He fears someone might poison his food. A chair, watched over by someone he trusts, also travels with him. This is to make sure Saddam does not sit on a poisoned tack stuck in a chair cushion.

GLORY AND RICHES

Saddam Hussein has a huge ego. After the Baath took control of the government in 1968, he demanded to be called "Mr. Deputy." He loves titles. When he became president, he took on four others: head of government, commander in chief of the armed forces, secretary-general of the Baath Party, and chairman of the Revolutionary Command Council. Saddam's birthday was made a national holiday in Iraq even though Moslems don't usually celebrate birthdays. Large portraits of Saddam appear all over Iraq. In Baghdad they are painted on buildings. A 60 foot statue of Saddam stands in the city center. In the official government media, he is glorified in songs and poems.

Saddam Hussein has a loyal following in Iraq.

As ruler of the country, he has access to large sums of money. After years of living in poverty, he wanted to enjoy life's luxuries. His clothes are tailored and made in Europe.

He also took a second wife. (Moslem men may have more than one wife.) However, the woman he wanted for his second wife, Samira Shahbandar, was already married. The tall blond woman was a member of a well-known Baghdad merchant family. Her husband did not protest. He later received a job promotion.

BLOODSHED

Soon after gaining total control over Iraq, Saddam took on his Western neighbor, Iran. After a series of border skirmishes, Iraq invaded Iran. Saddam feared the Iranians might try to export their Moslem fundamentalism where religious leaders applying a strict view of Islam dominate the government. Other Gulf nations shared that fear.

Saddam's military advisors told him Iran's armed forces would be easy to defeat. Although he had no army experience, Saddam directed the war himself. The war was anything but easy. Missiles rained on Baghdad. Some 200,000 Iraqi soldiers were lost. The bloody conflict lasted from 1980 until 1988 when a cease-fire was declared. The estimated cost of the war exceeded $110 billion.

Also in 1988, trouble arose at home. The long-standing hostility between the Kurdish tribes in northern Iraq and the Baghdad government erupted once again. Saddam sent troops with mustard gas to stop the uprising. Iraq became the first nation to use poison gas against its own citizens. An estimated 5,000 Kurds died.

Saddam directing the war and urging Iraqis to fight to the death.

THE MILLION-DOLLAR BUNKER

During the war with Iran, Saddam built an elaborate hiding place in Baghdad. His underground hideout cost $65 million to build in 1981.

The 12-room shelter was 50 feet below a guest house of Saddam's presidential palace. The walls were built to withstand a nuclear bomb. They were six feet thick and lined with lead. A three-ton steel door covered the main entrance.

A multitude of television screens and a broadcast studio enabled him to stay in contact with the outside world.

The underground fortress was not without its comforts. There was a sauna, a heated pool, a four-poster bed, and plush carpets.

During Operation Desert Storm in 1991, many officials believe Saddam again used this secret retreat.

Blueprint for a bunker

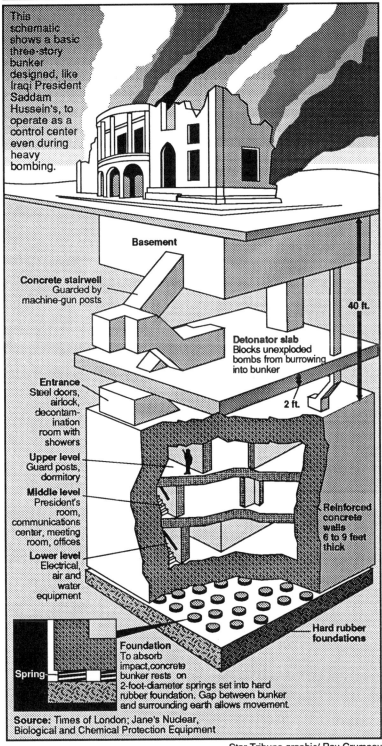

This schematic shows a basic three-story bunker designed, like Iraqi President Saddam Hussein's, to operate as a control center even during heavy bombing.

Basement

Concrete stairwell
Guarded by machine-gun posts

Detonator slab
Blocks unexploded bombs from burrowing into bunker

40 ft.

2 ft.

Entrance
Steel doors, airlock, decontamination room with showers

Upper level
Guard posts, dormitory

Middle level
President's room, communications center, meeting room, offices

Lower level
Electrical, air and water equipment

Reinforced concrete walls 6 to 9 feet thick

Hard rubber foundations

Foundation
To absorb impact, concrete bunker rests on 2-foot-diameter springs set into hard rubber foundation. Gap between bunker and surrounding earth allows movement.

Spring

Source: Times of London; Jane's Nuclear, Biological and Chemical Protection Equipment

Star Tribune graphic/ Ray Grumney

19

WHY DID SADDAM INVADE KUWAIT?

The word "Saddam" means "one who confronts."
Saddam Hussein has done so all his adult life. He
confronted his enemies on his rise to power. As
ruler of Iraq, he confronted Iran. Then in the
summer of 1990, Saddam decided to make the
small country of Kuwait, Iraq's "19th province." In
so doing, he perhaps unwittingly confronted a
powerful adversary, the United States of America.

No one may ever know why the hard-to-predict,
power-loving Saddam Hussein took over Kuwait.
Saddam had grown increasingly upset with the
neighboring Gulf states. Kuwait included. He
thought his Arab neighbors should be more
grateful to him for fighting Iran. Arguments over
the Iraq-Kuwait border had been going on for
decades.

However, the general agreement is that Saddam
moved on Kuwait to gain badly-needed cash.
During the 1980s, Iraq became an economic
disaster. There was a $70 or $80 billion debt from
the war with Iran. The cost of keeping almost six
percent of the population in the armed forces
$10 billion a year.

Much of the $70 billion was owed to Kuwait and
other Gulf states. No one expected that it ever

would be paid. In fact, in the summer of 1990 Saddam demanded more money from his neighbors, including another $27 billion from Kuwait alone. By July he threatened to use force if the money wasn't forthcoming. That same month, he moved thousands of his troops near the Iraqi border with Kuwait.

Yet no one in the region or the West thought he would actually take over Kuwait. But that is exactly what Iraq did on August 2, 1990. The Iraqis invaded Kuwait and took millions of dollars out of the country. Even stores were looted. Saddam's soldiers drove vehicles back across the border into Iraq.

Iraq invaded Kuwait leaving behind a trail of destruction.

A MISTAKEN BELIEF

Saddam probably believed no one would oppose his takeover. Saddam's brutal and aggressive conduct had been overlooked before. One analyst pointed out in early December 1990 that during the 1980s, "Hussein committed almost all of the same crimes against humanity that now outrage (President) Bush. Yet the Reagan and Bush administration did not threaten war — or even impose economic sanctions — against Saddam's regime.

"In fact, the United States took his side (in several instances)," the analyst noted. These were the years when "Washington had sought to improve its relationship with Baghdad despite Saddam's ruthless ambition," a newspaper noted.

"The Iraqi president clearly was convinced," the paper said, "that the West would not stand up to his aggression." This conviction "was based on years of personal observations."

Even as late as the end of July, Saddam thought the United States would ignore his invasion of Kuwait. The United States ambassador to Iraq told Saddam that this United States had "no opinion on the Arab-Arab conflicts, like your border disagreement with Kuwait." The ambassador said eight months later that the reflected U.S. policy. But, she said she emphasized that such conflicts must be settled peacefully.

Saddam Hussein made a mistake. There was instant opposition to his takeover of his tiny, oil-rich neighbor. President Bush had decided Saddam was now an enemy to be confronted . . . and defeated.

Saddam Hussein was considered extreme and dangerous.

A TOUGH OPPONENT?

During the military buildup that was Operation Desert Shield, Saddam was portrayed as a very tough opponent. He was described as "cunning, stubborn, and . . . fearless."

One Iraqi living in the U.S. who had studied Saddam said the fearlessness was probably his most important characteristic. Saddam, he said, "simply does not understand fear. He does not comprehend it. That is what makes him so dangerous."

Some Westerners who had studied Hussein said he was at his best when in trouble. They called him "cunning and resourceful" and warned early in the Gulf War: "Don't underestimate him."

Although an "extremist," Saddam was "dangerous and long-lasting" because he knew "when to stop." That had been the opinion expressed by a respected Middle East observer well over a year before the Gulf conflict.

American troops landing in Saudi Arabia in support of Operation Desert Shield.

SADDAM DEFEATED

But this cunning, dangerous adversary was defeated when Desert Shield turned to Desert Storm. Why didn't Saddam stop before the United States and coalition forces drove him out of Kuwait? Why did he hold onto Kuwait while allied planes caused massive damage in Baghdad and elsewhere in Iraq? Why did he wait as thousands of his troops were killed in the land war?

One theory is that Saddam believed he would win even if he lost on the battlefield. Four weeks into Operation Desert Storm, one analyst said that each day Saddam held out he became "more of a hero to many . . . Arab Moslems. You regularly hear people in the street counting the days Saddam has kept at bay the multinational forces led by the United States."

Arab Moslems generally regarded Hussein as one of the first Arab leaders to stand up to the West, according to the observer. These Arabs, he said, frowned on what they saw as the West's "materialist, secular, and imperialist ways."

Thus, hundreds of thousands of people from Cairo to Baghdad were expected to see Saddam as a hero even if he was defeated militarily.

An American soldier walks past the dead bodies of Iraqi soldiers. Kuwaiti oil wells burn in the background. All of Kuwait's 950 producing oil wells were either on fire or otherwise damaged by Iraqi sabatoge or allied bombing.

"Everywhere . . . he is regarded as a man who does what he says he will do," a magazine writer noted. "He said he would fire the Scuds at Tel Aviv (Israel) and he did. He said he would release the oil into the sea and he did. In the Middle East, that counts a great deal, even if you are defeated in the end."

Saddam also pictured himself as one who took from rich Arabs and gave to poor Arabs. The poor were by far the majority.

The cost of the Iraqi invasion was horrendous and everyone paid.

HORRENDOUS COSTS

Whatever his reasons, Saddam Hussein, during the Gulf War, put his nation through its second war in little more than a decade. The cost was horrendous. No figures were released on Iraqi casualties during Operation Desert Storm. However, thousands of soldiers and civilians were victims of the seven weeks of allied bombing that preceded the land offensive. There were estimates that about 80,000 Iraqi troops were killed before the fighting ceased on February 27, 1991.

There was also massive property damage in Baghdad and elsewhere in Iraq. The United States and the coalition forces considered bridges, roads, power stations, and sewage treatment plants military targets. The damage also created a public health crisis when water and sanitation devices became unavailable.

By February 22, Saddam accepted a Soviet peace proposal. He agreed to withdraw from Kuwait. But the Soviet plan did not embrace all the terms President Bush had set for ending the war. The United States did not want Saddam to return his undamaged weapons to Iraq and fight again at a later date. Moreover, said a State Department official, "one of our objectives is to humiliate him.

We don't want him to be able to claim a victory of any kind out of this." Iraqi forces still occupied Kuwait two days later when a new U.S. deadline for withdrawal passed.

United States President, George Bush.

"THE MOTHER OF ALL BATTLES" A ROUT

Saddam did not agree to the terms the United States set for his withdrawal from Kuwait, so allied forces launched a ground war on February 23, 1991. Many military officials feared that this would be a bloody battle. After all, Iraq had the world's fourth-largest army. In the flamboyant phrases Saddam often used, he predicted this would be "The Mother of All Battles."

Just after the land war began, Saddam urged his ground troops to fight to the death. If they failed, he said, "a lengthy darkness would prevail over Iraq." But he assured Iraqis that his troops would eventually win and that they would "show no mercy."

As it turned out, Saddam sent his troops into what one observer called, "the teeth of a vastly superior force." Perhaps it was one war too many for Saddam's forces. Heavy damage had been inflicted on the Iraqi forces by the constant bombing. When the allied troops advanced into Kuwait and Iraq, the Iraqis for the most part showed little will to fight. They surrendered at an astonishing rate — an estimated 75,000 in less than five days. Those that did fight were overrun.

Murals of Iraq's president are seen throughout Baghdad.

Saddam's troops were humiliated. He soon ordered their withdrawal even though no cease-fire existed.

President Bush called off the attack after 100 hours. Iraq's half-a-million-member army had been routed. On February 27, the United States president went on televison to say he was halting offensive military action in the Gulf.

On March 3, Iraqi generals met with military representatives of the victors and agreed to the surrender terms presented to them. The terms included an immediate exchange of all prisoners of war. Iraq agreed to help locate mines it had placed in Kuwait. Iraq also agreed to comply with the terms of the March 3rd United Nations Security Council resolution. The U.N. said Iraq must renounce their annexation of Kuwait, stop all hostile acts, and pay war reparations.

Despite the crushing defeat, Saddam's government continued to heap praise and glory on their nation's warriors. Saddam, too, was praised. In early March, posters went up in Baghdad proclaiming Saddam "the son of all Iraqi mothers."

And he was still in power in Iraq. A U.S. newspaper reported one reason for Saddam remaining in power. The newspaper wrote that many Iraqi citizens thought that President Bush wanted to destroy Iraq. "Almost no one, " reported the paper, "appears to believe Bush's statement that the United States has no differences with the Iraqi people, only their leadership."

"Even if we know deep in our hearts that Saddam is to blame, how can that justify this destruction?" asked one resident of the capital, referring to the damage done by the bombing. "We will understand why the army is destroyed, but why the bridges and roads?"

MORE TROUBLE FOR SADDAM

After the Gulf War ended, the 53-year-old Saddam faced another problem: unrest at home.

In southern Iraq the dissenters were Shiite Moslem fundamentalists. The Shiites represent about 60 percent of the nation's population. The majority live in the south. The Shiites have long resented the Baath Party's control of the Nation.

The aftermath of the war, Baghdad, Iraq.

(The party is dominated by Sunni Moslems, who represent only 20 percent of the population.)

There was also unrest in the north, where the Kurds once again showed their opposition to Saddam's ruling party.

Roadblocks went up around Baghdad.

As a result of the turmoil, most Western journalists were told to leave Iraq in early March 1991. The departing news correspondents reported widespread discontent in Baghdad because of the results of the futile war with the United States and its allies. "Down, Down Saddam" had been painted on a wall, for example. This was a daring act in Iraq.

A SURVIVOR

For many years, Saddam had survived numerous plots against him. It was generally agreed that Saddam would crush the post-war unrest. For one thing, there was little organized opposition to his regime. He still held tight control of the population, enabling him to stifle those who might try to mount an organized campaign against him.

An Iraqi Kurd searches for a place to pitch his tent. Some 250,000 Kurds fled Iraq and are in this mountainous camp along the Turkey boarder with Iraq.

37

The Iraqi president took steps to keep the military loyal to him. His Central Command Council ordered pardons for soldiers who had deserted during the Gulf War. (Deserting soldiers had been executed in the Iraq-Iran war.) Saddam also reportedly paid cash bonuses to loyal troops.

Saddam also put a trusted cousin in charge of internal security. As one reporter wrote, "There's no denying Saddam's skill in holding fast power in Iraq."

By late March 1991, in Washington, the Bush administration was worried about what would happen if Saddam should fall, although earlier President Bush had asked the Iraqis to oust Saddam. Now the United States feared that his fall could result in a breakup of the country. Another negative result could be the rise of religious fundamentalists linked to Iran.

A *New York Times* columnist wrote in late March that a united Iraq "may represent the only chance for its people to be at peace with each other and with their neighbors.

Palestinians and other foreign nationals of Kuwait line up for bread and food outside a local supermarket. Large clouds of smoke caused by hundreds of burning oil wells continue to block out the sun, making day seem like night.

On March 26, the Bush administration indicated that the United States would not come to the aid of any of the groups within Iraq rebelling against Saddam. Newspapers quoted a senior administration official saying that President Bush "has no, I mean absolutely no intention, of putting the United States into the middle of a civil war (in Iraq)." Eventually, U.S. troops did move into border areas where hundreds of thousands of Kurds and Shiites fled. American soldiers helped establish refugee camps in Turkey in what was called Operation Provide Comfort.

Saddam continues to be supported by his allies.